August

Julie Murray

Abdo
MONTHS
Kids

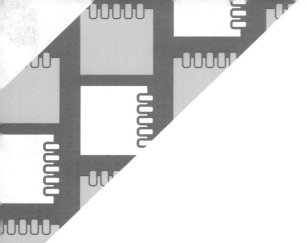

abdopublishing.com

Published by Abdo Kids, a division of ABDO, PO Box 398166, Minneapolis, Minnesota 55439.
Copyright © 2018 by Abdo Consulting Group, Inc. International copyrights reserved in all countries.
No part of this book may be reproduced in any form without written permission from the publisher.

Printed in the United States of America, North Mankato, Minnesota.

052017

092017

THIS BOOK CONTAINS
RECYCLED MATERIALS

Photo Credits: iStock, Shutterstock

Production Contributors: Teddy Borth, Jennie Forsberg, Grace Hansen

Design Contributors: Christina Doffing, Candice Keimig, Dorothy Toth

Publisher's Cataloging in Publication Data

Names: Murray, Julie, 1969-, author.

Title: August / by Julie Murray.

Description: Minneapolis, Minnesota : Abdo Kids, 2018 | Series: Months |
    Includes bibliographical references and index.

Identifiers: LCCN 2016962339 | ISBN 9781532100222 (lib. bdg.) |
    ISBN 9781532100918 (ebook) | ISBN 9781532101465 (Read-to-me ebook)

Subjects: LCSH: August (Month)--Juvenile literature. | Calendar--Juvenile literature.

Classification: DDC 398/.33--dc23

LC record available at http://lccn.loc.gov/2016962339

Table of Contents

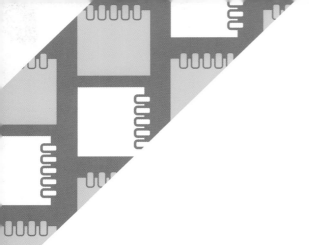

August

There are 12 months in the year.

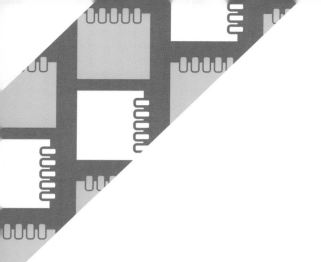

August is the 8th month.

It has 31 days.

August

1	2	3	4	5	6	7
8	9	10	11	12	13	14
15	16	17	18	19	20	21
22	23	24	25	26	27	28
29	30	31				

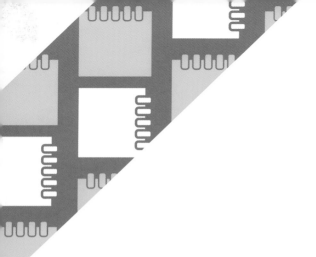

The days are hot! Ivan swims at the beach.

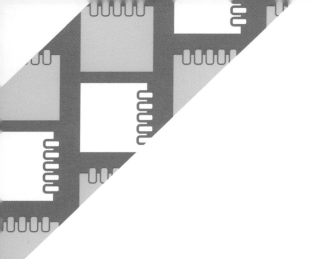

Kara plays tennis.

She wins the point!

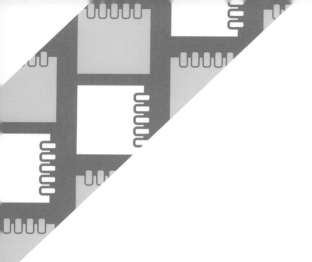

Cole rides in the boat.

He enjoys the lake.

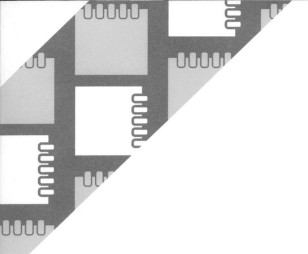

Mary is on the plane. Her family is going on a trip.

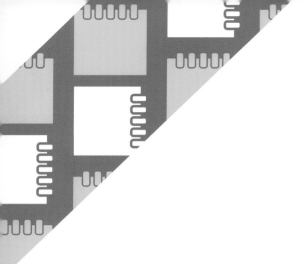

Camila sees a snake.

She is at the zoo.

17

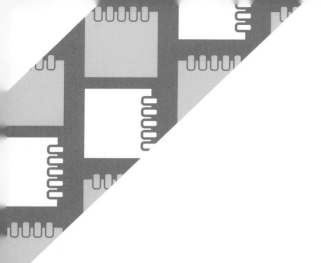

It's back to school for many kids. Nina gets her supplies.

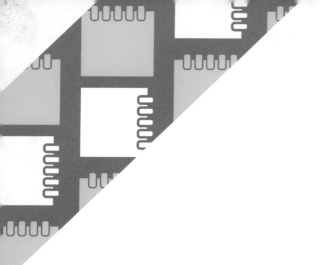

Ally is ready for school.

She loves August!

Fun Days in August

National Watermelon Day
August 3

Coast Guard Day
August 4

National Aviation Day
August 19

National Waffle Day
August 24

Glossary

point
the smallest unit of scoring in tennis. Four points win a game.

supplies
materials needed for a certain thing.

Index

abdokids.com

Use this code to log on to abdokids.com and access crafts, games, videos, and more!

Abdo Kids Code: MAKO222